YEARS OF SLAVERY

BY JIM OLLHOFF

Published by ABDO Publishing Company, 8000 West 78th Street, Suite 310, Edina, MN 55439. Copyright ©2011 by Abdo Consulting Group, Inc. International copyrights reserved in all countries. No part of this book may be reproduced in any form without written permission from the publisher. ABDO & Daughters™ is a trademark and logo of ABDO Publishing Company.

Printed in the United States of America, North Mankato, Minnesota.
112010
012011

♻ PRINTED ON RECYCLED PAPER

Editor: John Hamilton
Graphic Design: John Hamilton
Cover Design: Neil Klinepier
Cover Photo: Getty Images
Interior Photos and Illustrations: AP-pgs 22, 23, 29; Architect of the Capitol-pg 26; Corbis-pgs 10-11, 13, 15, 16-17, 19, 20, 25, 28; Getty Images-pgs 8, 9, 18, 21, 24; Granger Collection-pg 13; iStockphoto-pgs 4-5; National Geographic-pgs 6-7, 12.

Library of Congress Cataloging-in-Publication Data

Ollhoff, Jim, 1959-
    Years of slavery / Jim Ollhoff.
        p. cm. -- (African-American history)
    Includes index.
    ISBN 978-1-61714-714-2
    1. Slavery--United States--History--Juvenile literature. 2. African Americans--History. I. Title.
    E441.O55 2011
    973.7'1--dc22
                            2010038741

CONTENTS

Slavery in the World 4

Slavery Begins in the New World 6

Why Did the New World Need Slaves? 10

The Triangle Trade 14

Slavery in the United States 16

Life as a Slave 20

Escaping Slavery 22

The Underground Railroad 24

Hopes for Freedom 26

Glossary 30

Index 32

SLAVERY
IN THE
WORLD

Slavery has been a common practice in the world since history began. Almost every culture has had slavery. Slaves were often prisoners of war. If people borrowed money and could not pay it back, they sometimes became slaves. Sometimes children of abandoned parents became slaves. Slavery has existed for as long as humans have roamed the land.

Slavery, in fact, continues to exist today. Even though almost every country in the world has laws against it, slavery persists. People continue to be owned by others, working in terrible conditions for little or no pay.

But there was something different about African slavery in the New World. For perhaps the first time, slavery was based on skin color instead of the enslavement of a defeated enemy, or because a person couldn't repay a loan. In North America, from the 1500s to 1865, most slaves were people from Africa who had dark skin.

SLAVERY BEGINS IN THE NEW WORLD

The European slave trade began around 1440. Men from Portugal captured Africans and sold them in Lisbon, the capital of Portugal. Within 10 years, the Portuguese were kidnapping and selling 1,000 Africans per year.

The Europeans had better weapons than the Africans. At first, the Europeans captured the slaves themselves. Soon, it became more profitable to pay some African kingdoms to bring slaves to the coast. Armed with European weapons, they went to war against other African kingdoms. They captured and brought prisoners to the west African coast, where European ships picked them up. Some Africans made big profits by selling people from other African kingdoms to the Europeans.

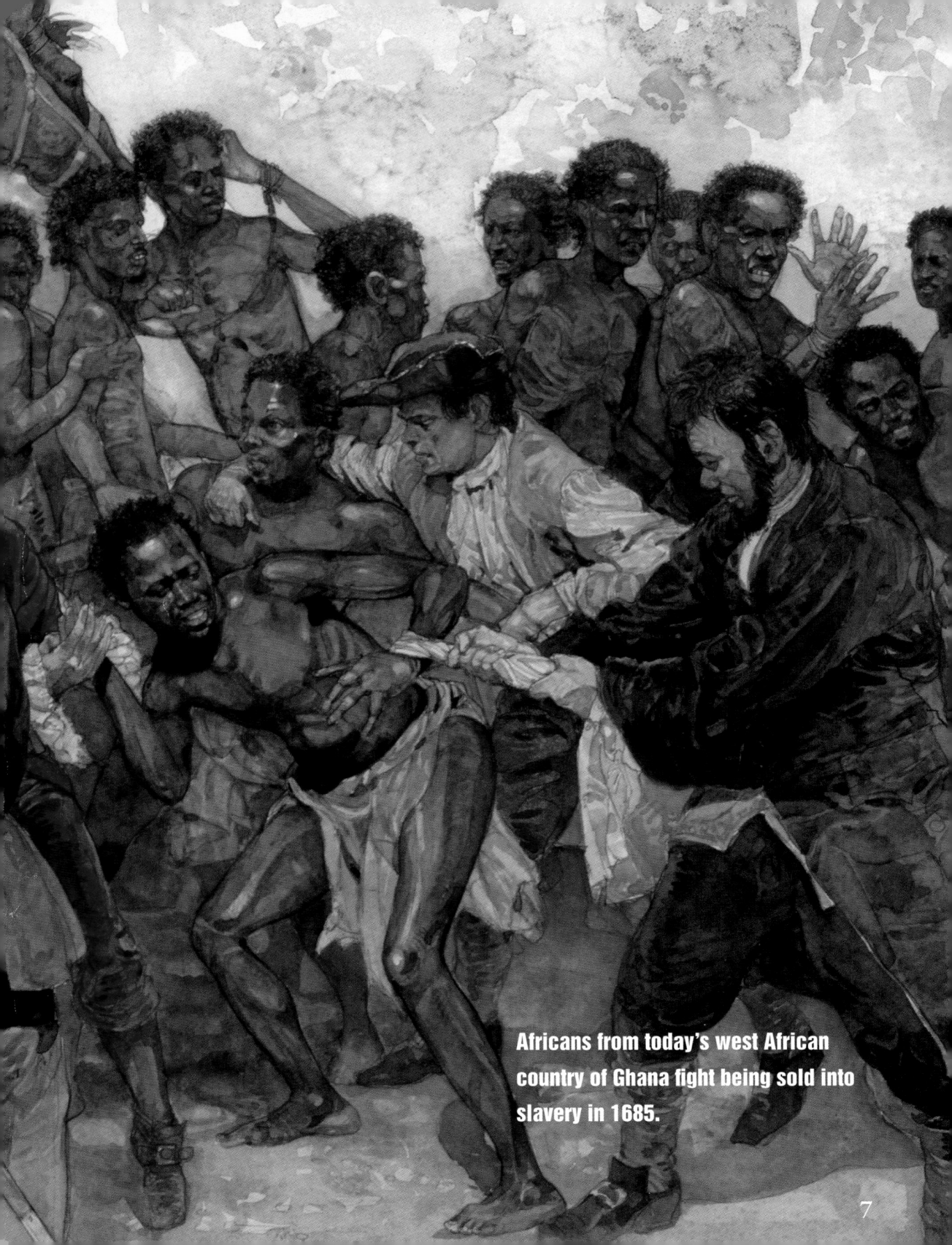

Africans from today's west African country of Ghana fight being sold into slavery in 1685.

A sugar plantation *on the Caribbean island of Martinique. An overseer on horseback directs cutters in the cane field. In the 1500s, the demand for sugar skyrocketed. To fill the need for cheap labor, slaves were brought from Africa.*

Christopher Columbus arrived in the islands of the Caribbean in 1492. By 1501, the governor of Hispaniola (today's Haiti and the Dominican Republic) already wanted slave labor. Hispaniola had become a large producer of sugar, which required a lot of workers. The Portuguese bought more slaves from Africa. They sold the slaves to Spain, and Spain sold them to Hispaniola. It was a horrible trafficking of human beings that continued for more than 300 years.

By the time the Pilgrims landed on Plymouth Rock (on the shore of today's state of Massachusetts) in 1620, there were already 300,000 Africans in the New World. Most were in Brazil, Mexico, and the islands of the Caribbean. Slaves were used as bricklayers, blacksmiths, and farmhands on the large plantations.

Phrenology was the false belief that intelligence can be determined by the shape of someone's skull. It led to a form of scientific racism.

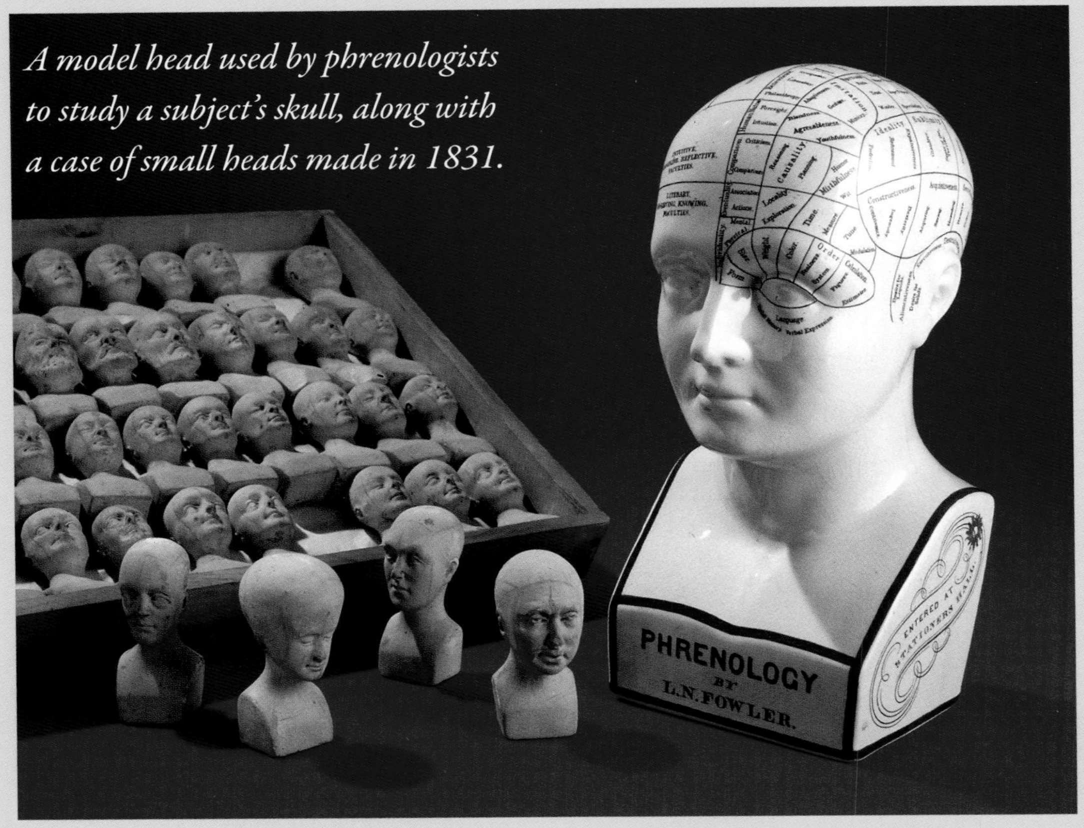

A model head used by phrenologists to study a subject's skull, along with a case of small heads made in 1831.

Samuel George Morton (1799–1851)

Physician Samuel George Morton lived in Philadelphia, Pennsylvania. He studied human skulls. He believed in phrenology, the idea that personality could be measured by the size and shape of a person's head.

Morton measured the skulls of Africans, Native Americans, Asians, and Europeans. He decided, based on the shape of the skulls, that Europeans, or people with white skin, had superior intelligence. Africans, he believed, had low intelligence. This idea, called scientific racism, helped justify slavery in America. Morton's work was not scientific at all, but at the time it sounded like real science.

Morton

Today, scientists know there is no relationship between intelligence and skin color or skull shape.

WHY DID THE NEW WORLD NEED SLAVES?

Settling the New World took a lot of hard labor. As slavery spread into the English colonies of North America, as well as Brazil and Mexico, people wanted slaves for almost everything. In the southern colonies, large cotton and tobacco plantations were growing fast. These crops needed a lot of care at every stage of production. Many plantation owners felt that the only way to make a profit was with slave labor. Profit was—and still is—more important to many people than human life and dignity.

The northern colonies didn't have as many large plantations. The North had more industry. It didn't need as many slaves. There was still some slavery in the North, but the South had much more because of the large plantations.

African American slaves working on a Southern cotton plantation. The labor-intensive cotton, sugar, and tobacco industries used slave labor to be more profitable.

Captured African slaves in 1685, waiting to be shipped to the New World.

There was a brief attempt to enslave Native Americans. However, the Native Americans knew the land, and they knew the languages of the nearby tribes, so they could work together to escape slave traders. It was also difficult to identify them from far away, because their skin color was similar to the Europeans. Also, the Native Americans were often sick with European diseases, such as smallpox.

From the slaveholders' point of view, there were advantages to African slaves. There seemed to be a never-ending supply of slave ships coming from the African continent. The Africans were easy to identify because of their black skin. Also, most didn't understand the English language when they first arrived. They were often grouped together with other slaves who were not from the same areas in Africa, so the slaves couldn't even speak to each other. That made it much easier for the slave owners to control the African slaves.

Benjamin Banneker

Black Heritage USA 15c

In 1980, the U.S. Postal Service issued a 15-cent commemorative stamp honoring astronomer and mathematician Benjamin Banneker during the nationwide observance of Black History month. Banneker was a pioneer American scientist and mathematician.

Benjamin Banneker (1731–1806)

Benjamin Banneker was a free African American who was the descendant of slaves. He was probably born in Maryland. He was interested in science, especially astronomy. He became friends with Peter Heinrichs, a Quaker who opened up his library to Banneker, who was eager to learn.

Banneker became an important scientist of his time. He created one of the first clocks in America. He wrote about solar eclipses, the times for sunrises and sunsets, and phases of the moon. He also exchanged letters with Thomas Jefferson, the writer of the Declaration of Independence, about the injustice of owning slaves.

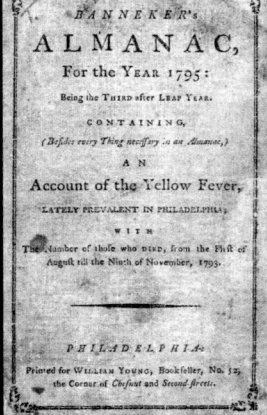

Benjamin Banneker's almanac for the year 1795.

THE TRIANGLE TRADE

The slave trade to America is sometimes called the Triangle Trade because of the shape of the routes that slave ships traveled. Starting in England, ships were loaded with cloth, beads, rum, salt, and guns, and then set sail for western Africa. The ships's cargo was then traded for slaves. The ships, loaded with slaves, traveled to the Americas.

The slaves were sold, and then the ships were loaded with sugar, molasses, tobacco, and other raw materials. The ships then made their way back to England, where the raw materials were sold, and the cycle would start all over again.

If the weather was good, the route from Africa to the Americas took 6 to 10 weeks. The Africans were shackled together in horribly cramped conditions. There was no sanitation. Smallpox, dysentery, and other diseases were common. Up to one-third of the Africans died on each trip because of the cramped and unsanitary conditions. Their bodies were thrown overboard.

A simplified map of the Triangle Trade, which was a web of trade routes between Europe, Africa, and the New World.

Sugar, molasses, tobacco, and other raw materials

Cloth, beads, rum, salt, and guns

Slaves

An illustration of a tightly packed slave ship. Many African slaves died during the long voyage to the New World aboard overcrowded and unsanitary ships.

SLAVERY IN THE UNITED STATES

Slavery began in what would become the United States in the early 1600s (the states were British colonies until 1776). At first, the slaves were more like indentured servants. This meant that the slaves worked for a period of time, often four to seven years. After this time, they were granted freedom, along with land and food. However, indentured servitude was short-lived.

Before the 1640s, many laws declared that only non-Christians could be slaves. But over time, new laws and regulations shifted the definition of slavery.

In the 1640s, laws began to appear that stated people with white skin could not be slaves. By the late 1600s, it was clear that slavery was based not on religion, but on skin color.

Slave leg blocks *at Kingsley Plantation on Fort George Island in Florida. Today, the plantation is a national historic site.*

By 1680, it was no longer a crime to kill a slave who resisted doing work. These kinds of laws, one by one and state by state, created the horrific institution known as slavery.

By 1700, there was no question that the American colonies had become a slave society, and England had become the main provider of slaves. By the early 1700s, blacks outnumbered whites in many colonies. People in the white society began to fear that they would be overwhelmed and attacked by the slaves. Laws and punishments became stricter. After a slave revolt in the 1750s, it became a crime to teach slaves how to read or write.

In New England, there were fewer slaves than in the southern states. Still, New England had 13,000 slaves by the 1750s. After the Revolutionary War, most of the northern states outlawed slavery. However, small pockets of slavery lingered in the North for 100 years because of poor law enforcement.

By 1790, slaves included one of every five Americans. By 1800, there were about one million slaves. By 1861, the start of the Civil War, the number of Americans in slavery had grown to about four million.

Shackles used to
restrain Africans
sold into slavery.

19

LIFE AS A SLAVE

Slave children were sent to work in the fields as early as age five or six.
Slaves started work before sunrise. Men called slave drivers were responsible for getting the slaves to the fields and overseeing their work. Toiling in tobacco, cotton, or rice fields was backbreaking work. Whippings and other kinds of punishments were common. The slaves worked all day, with only a few short breaks for meals. When the sun went down, they fed the farm animals, chopped wood, and mended their clothes. They spent much of the time chained with shackles so they couldn't escape.

Some slaves, usually women, worked in the house of the slave owner. They cared for the slave owner's children, cooked food, and cleaned house.

Slave families were often broken up and sold separately, so children, mothers, and fathers wound up in different places. There was little mercy shown to Africans and their pleas to keep their families together.

A slave family working on a cotton plantation near Savannah, Georgia. Many families were sold to different owners and split up.

A young boy working in a cotton field in South Carolina. Slaves were sent to work in the fields at a very young age.

ESCAPING SLAVERY

There were a few ways for slaves to gain their freedom. Sometimes, with permission from the slave owners, slaves could make extra money doing odd jobs. After earning enough money, the slaves could buy their own freedom.

This didn't happen very often, but it was possible for some. Sometimes, slave owners granted freedom to slaves. It might have been out of gratitude for good service, or because the slave owner had a change of heart about the morality of slavery. Sometimes, a female slave and the slave owner fell in love, and so the slave owner granted the slave her freedom.

Nat Turner led a slave revolt in 1831 in Virginia that resulted in dozens of deaths. This illustration shows Turner's capture. He was later executed.

Another way to freedom was to escape. This involved running away from the slave owners, and then evading capture as the slaves fled northward. The escaping slaves would try to make it to the free states in the North. If they were caught, they would suffer terrible punishment, and possibly be killed.

Sometimes, slaves tried to gain freedom by revolting. A Virginia slave named Nat Turner led a large revolt in 1831. At least 40 slaves eventually joined Turner. By the time the fighting came to an end, more than 50 white people were murdered. Turner was captured and executed, along with dozens of other rebels who had joined the uprising. And for a time following the revolt, angry white mobs murdered approximately 200 African Americans who had nothing to do with the rebellion.

THE UNDERGROUND RAILROAD

The Underground Railroad wasn't a railroad, and it wasn't underground. It was a network of secret routes and safe houses where runaway slaves could make their way to the free states of the North.

Former slave William Still is often considered the father of the Underground Railroad. He and other free blacks, along with anti-slavery whites, created the network in the early 1800s. It reached its peak in the 1850s. Historians say as many as 100,000 slaves used the Underground Railroad to escape to the northern states and Canada.

Many routes were used, including boats. No one person knew the entire operation. Each group used a small part of the route. Safe houses where slaves could hide were called "stations" and "depots." The owner of a safe house was called a "station master." The "conductor" took slaves from one location to another.

The Cincinnati, Ohio, home of Levi Coffin, a Quaker abolitionist. The house was used as a stop along the Underground Railroad.

Harriet Tubman (center, in blue) escorting escaped slaves into Canada.

Harriet Tubman (1820?–1913)

Harriet Tubman was one of the most famous conductors of the Underground Railroad. She was born a slave in Maryland. As an adult, she escaped to freedom by running away to Philadelphia, Pennsylvania.

After gaining her freedom, Tubman helped other slaves escape by using the Underground Railroad. She helped at least 70 slaves find freedom in the northern states and Canada. During the Civil War, she worked as a nurse, scout, and spy.

Tubman and many other escaped slaves spoke and wrote about their experiences. These stories helped to turn the tide of popular opinion against slavery.

HOPES FOR FREEDOM

Several events gave hope to slaves that freedom would eventually come. In 1776, the Declaration of Independence was adopted. Future President Thomas Jefferson was the primary writer of the document. In it, he wrote the famous words, "All men are created equal." Thomas Jefferson owned 202 slaves when he wrote those words.

While the Declaration of Independence didn't give freedom to slaves, the idea that everyone was created equal was a powerful one. Black and white authors frequently used those words in anti-slavery writings. Court cases that challenged the legality of slavery often referred to the statement that "all men are created equal."

Thomas Jefferson presents the Declaration of Independence to the Second Continental Congress on June 28, 1776, in this painting by John Trumbull. Today, the painting can be seen in the Capitol Rotunda, in Washington, DC.

When the United States declared its independence, England went to war to keep its colonies. During the Revolutionary War (1775–1783), slavery became an issue for both sides.

At first, George Washington, who commanded the American forces, didn't want blacks to fight. But then, the British governor of Virginia suggested that slaves might go free if they fought for the British. So, many slaves joined the British forces. Then, George Washington said that black slaves could fight in certain United States regiments. While the black fighters in the

In 1791, slaves in Haiti rebelled against French forces and eventually won independence, giving hope to the anti-slavery movement in the United States.

Revolutionary War didn't earn their freedom, the idea of "fighting for freedom" continued to be a powerful inspiration.

Another event that gave black slaves hope was the slave rebellion in the French colony of Haiti in 1791. There was a massive, violent slave rebellion that ended with a new president of Haiti—himself a former slave. Slavery was outlawed in Haiti, and the French military, under Napoléon Bonaparte, could not retake the country.

The anti-slavery movement became more widespread in the late 1700s and early 1800s. It was strongest in the North, but present everywhere. People openly discussed how cruel and immoral it was to own other human beings. Anti-slavery organizations were formed, conventions were held, and emotions became hotter.

Slave owners continued to press for slavery, and anti-slavery supporters continued to push for freedom. The two sides were on a collision course.

First Lady Michelle Obama applauds during the unveiling of a statue of Sojourner Truth in the Emancipation Hall of the U.S. Capitol, Washington, DC, April 28, 2009.

Sojourner Truth (1797?–1883)

Isabella Baumfree was born into slavery around 1797 in the state of New York. She grew up to be a very religious woman. In 1826, she escaped slavery. She changed her name to Sojourner Truth in 1843. She gave many speeches around the country, speaking out against slavery and supporting women's rights.

Before 1865, carriages in Washington, DC, did not have to stop for black riders. In 1865, a law was passed requiring carriages to carry blacks also. However, many carriage drivers refused to follow the law. Sojourner Truth demanded a ride on a carriage, and after a crowd gathered in support of her, the carriage was forced to stop. She refused to get off the carriage when the driver demanded she leave. Later, she made sure the driver was fired. She helped to bring about enforcement of the carriage laws.

GLOSSARY

ABOLITIONIST

A person who opposed slavery.

COLONY

A place, usually occupied by settlers, that is under the control of another country. Colonies were often created to benefit the mother country, usually by sending back needed raw materials such as crops, minerals, or lumber.

HISPANIOLA

A large island in the Caribbean Sea. Today it is split into two countries, Haiti and the Dominican Republic.

INDENTURED SERVANT

Someone who worked without pay for a certain length of time, in some cases four to seven years. After this time, they would be granted freedom.

NEW WORLD

After the early expeditions of European explorers, North and South America were referred to as the New World.

PHRENOLOGY

The now-discredited practice of classifying the size and shape of people's heads in order to measure their intelligence.

Plantation

A large farm where crops such as tobacco, sugar cane, and cotton are grown. It takes many people to run a plantation. Workers usually live right on the property. Early plantation owners in the New World used cheap slave labor to make their operations more profitable.

Quaker

A Christian denomination that emphasizes nonviolence. Officially called the Religious Society of Friends, many Quakers were abolitionists who demanded an end to slavery.

Revolutionary War (1775–1783)

A time when the United States fought for independence from England, and England went to war to keep its colony.

Smallpox

A very contagious disease, caused by a virus, that results in high fever, a rash, and fluid-filled blisters called pustules. Before modern medicine wiped out the disease in the 1970s, millions of people died from smallpox.

Triangle Trade

A way to describe the slave trade, because of the shape of the route that slave ships traveled. The ships started in England, landed in western Africa to pick up slaves, then went to the Americas, then back to England.

Underground Railroad

A large network of secret routes and safe houses that worked to transport runaway slaves to freedom in the northern states or Canada.

INDEX

A

Africa 5, 8, 12, 14
America 9, 13, 14

B

Banneker, Benjamin 13
Baumfree, Isabella 29
Brazil 8, 10

C

Canada 24, 25
Caribbean 8
Civil War 18, 25
Columbus, Christopher 8

D

Declaration of
    Independence 13, 26
Dominican Republic 8

E

England 14, 18, 28

H

Haiti 8, 28
Heinrichs, Peter 13
Hispaniola 8

J

Jefferson, Thomas 13, 26

L

Lisbon, Portugal 6

M

Maryland 13, 25
Massachusetts 8
Mexico 8, 10
Morton, Samuel George 9

N

Napoléon Bonaparte 28
New England 18
New World 5, 8, 10
North (United States) 10,
    18, 23, 24, 28
North America 5, 10

P

Philadelphia, PA 9, 25
phrenology 9
Pilgrims 8
Plymout Rock 8
Portugal 6

R

Revolutionary War 18, 28

S

scientific racism 9
South (United States) 10
Spain 8
Still, William 24

T

Triangle Trade 14
Truth, Sojourner 29
Tubman, Harriet 25
Turner, Nat 23

U

Underground Railroad
    24, 25
United States 16, 28

V

Virginia 23, 28

W

Washington, DC 29
Washington, George 28